Alfred's
INSTRUMENTAL
PLAY-ALONG

Favorite HYMNS
INSTRUMENTAL SOLOS

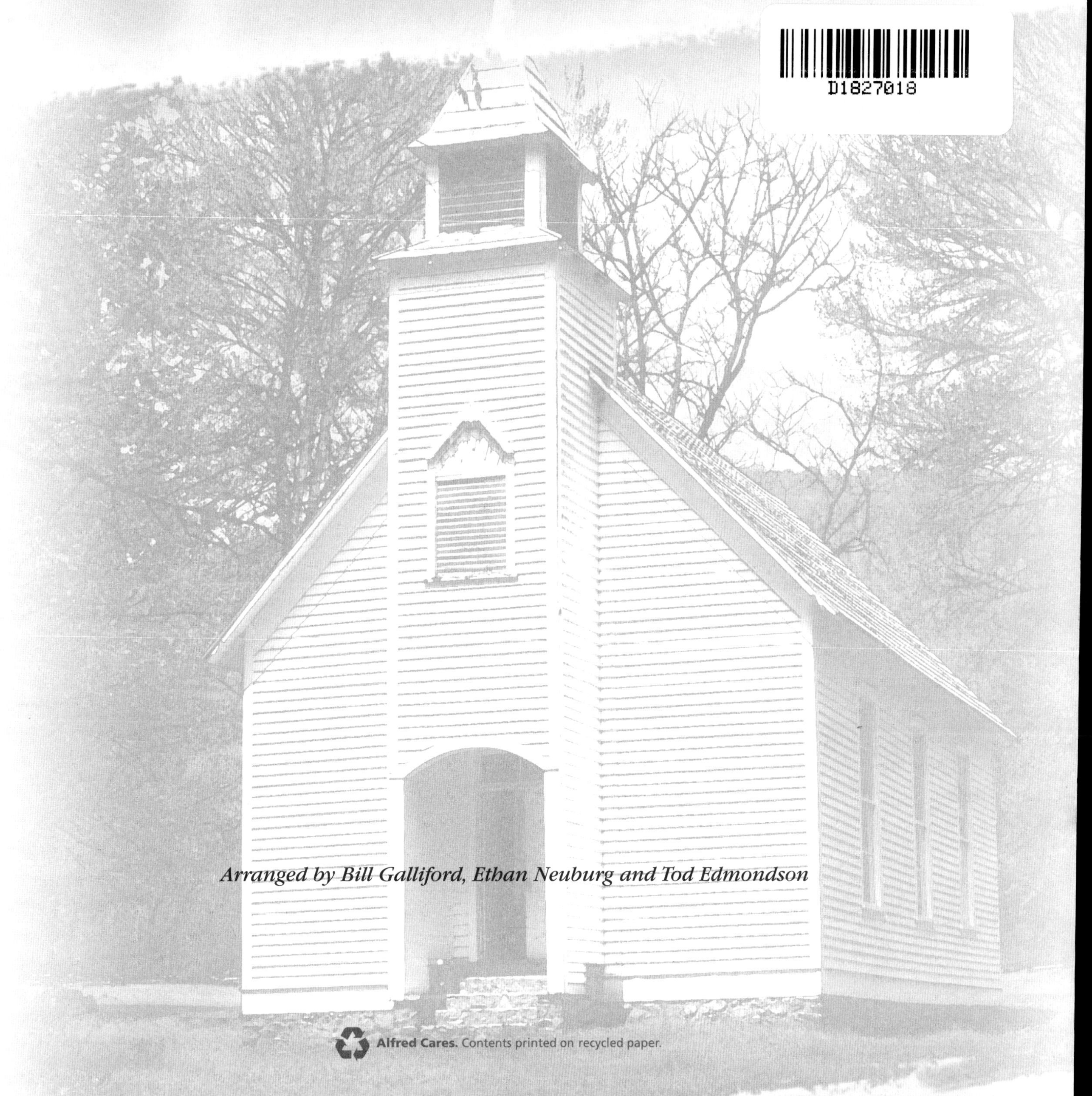

Arranged by Bill Galliford, Ethan Neuburg and Tod Edmondson

Alfred Cares. Contents printed on recycled paper.

Alfred

ISBN-10: 0-7390-7176-9
ISBN-13: 978-0-7390-7176-2

Photograph courtesy of Barry Erra

Contents

Track 2: Demo
Track 3: Play Along

AMAZING GRACE

TRADITIONAL AMERICAN MELODY

36112

ALL CREATURES OF OUR GOD AND KING

Track 4: Demo
Track 5: Play Along

By St. FRANCIS of ASSISI and
GEISTLICHE KIRCHENGESANGE, COLOGNE

Moderately ♩ = 76

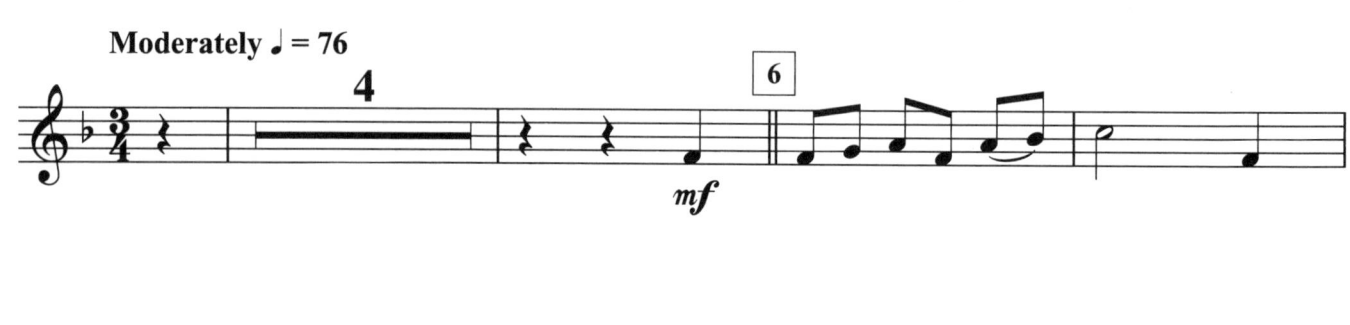

36112

HOLY, HOLY, HOLY! LORD GOD ALMIGHTY

Track 6: Demo
Track 7: Play Along

By JOHN B. DYKES
and REGINAL HEBER

Moderately slow, flowing ♩ = 88

JOYFUL, JOYFUL, WE ADORE THEE

Track 8: Demo
Track 9: Play Along

By HENRY VAN DYKE
and LUDWIG VAN BEETHOVEN

Moderately, majestically ♩ = 108

Take My Life and Let It Be

by

WOLFGANG AMADEUS MOZART

Lyrics by: FRANCES RIDLEY HAVERGAL

Published Under License From

Musicnotes, Inc.

Authorized for use by *Sarah Palmer*

 musicnotes.com

Take My Life and Let It Be

Words by
Frances R. Havergal

Music by
Wolfgang Amadeus Mozart

Authorized for use by: *Sarah Palmer*

A MIGHTY FORTRESS IS OUR GOD

Track 10: Demo
Track 11: Play Along

By MARTIN LUTHER

8

Track 12: Demo
Track 13: Play Along

BE THOU MY VISION

Moderately ♩ = 104

TRADITIONAL IRISH HYMN

IT IS WELL WITH MY SOUL

By HORATIO G. SPAFFORD
and PHILIP P. BLISS

Track 14: Demo
Track 15: Play Along

Moderate gospel feel ♩ = 104

GREAT IS THY FAITHFULNESS

Track 16: Demo
Track 17: Play Along

Music by
WILLIAM M. RUNYAN

Moderately, lilting ♩ = 96

HIS EYE IS ON THE SPARROW

Track 18: Demo
Track 19: Play Along

By CIVILLA D. MARTIN
and CHARLES H. GABRIEL

Gently, with expression (♩ = 108)

His Eye Is on the Sparrow - 2 - 1
36112

HOW GREAT THOU ART

Track 20: Demo
Track 21: Play Along

Words and Music by
STUART K. HINE

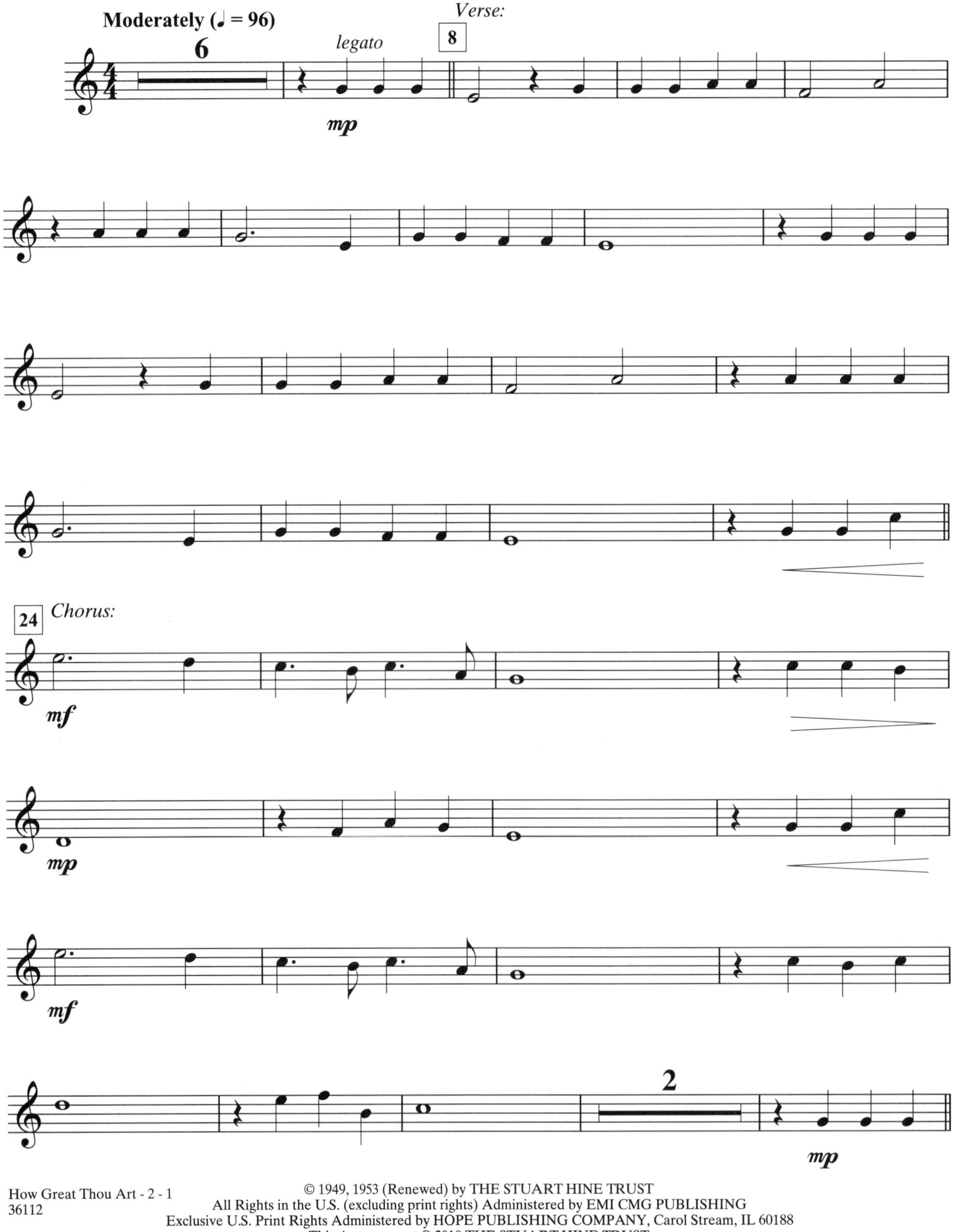

Moderately (♩ = 96)

legato

Verse:

Chorus:

O THE DEEP, DEEP LOVE OF JESUS

Track 22: Demo
Track 23: Play Along

By SAMUEL TREVOR FRANCIS
and THOMAS J. WILLIAMS

O the Deep, Deep Love of Jesus - 2 - 1
36112

'TIS SO SWEET TO TRUST IN JESUS

Track 24: Demo
Track 25: Play Along

By LOUISA M. R. STEAD
and WILLIAM J. KIRKPATRICK

Moderate folk style (♩ = 82)

36112

PARTS OF A CLARINET AND FINGERING CHART

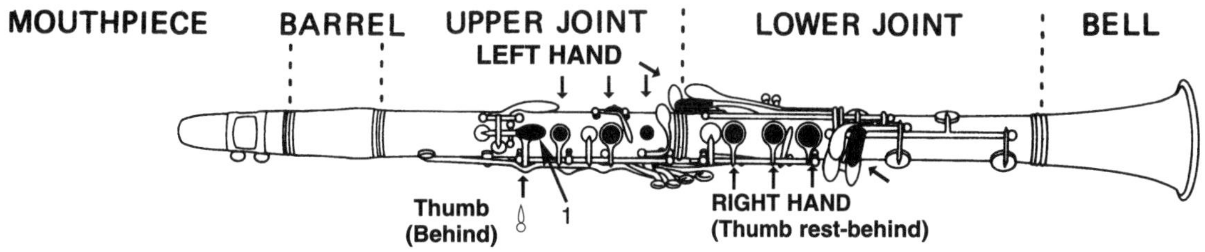
MOUTHPIECE
BARREL
UPPER JOINT
LEFT HAND
LOWER JOINT
BELL
Thumb
(Behind)
1
RIGHT HAND
(Thumb rest-behind)

● = press the key or cover the hole with your finger.
○ = do not press the key or cover the hole.

When there is more than one fingering given for a note, use the first one unless the alternate fingering is suggested.

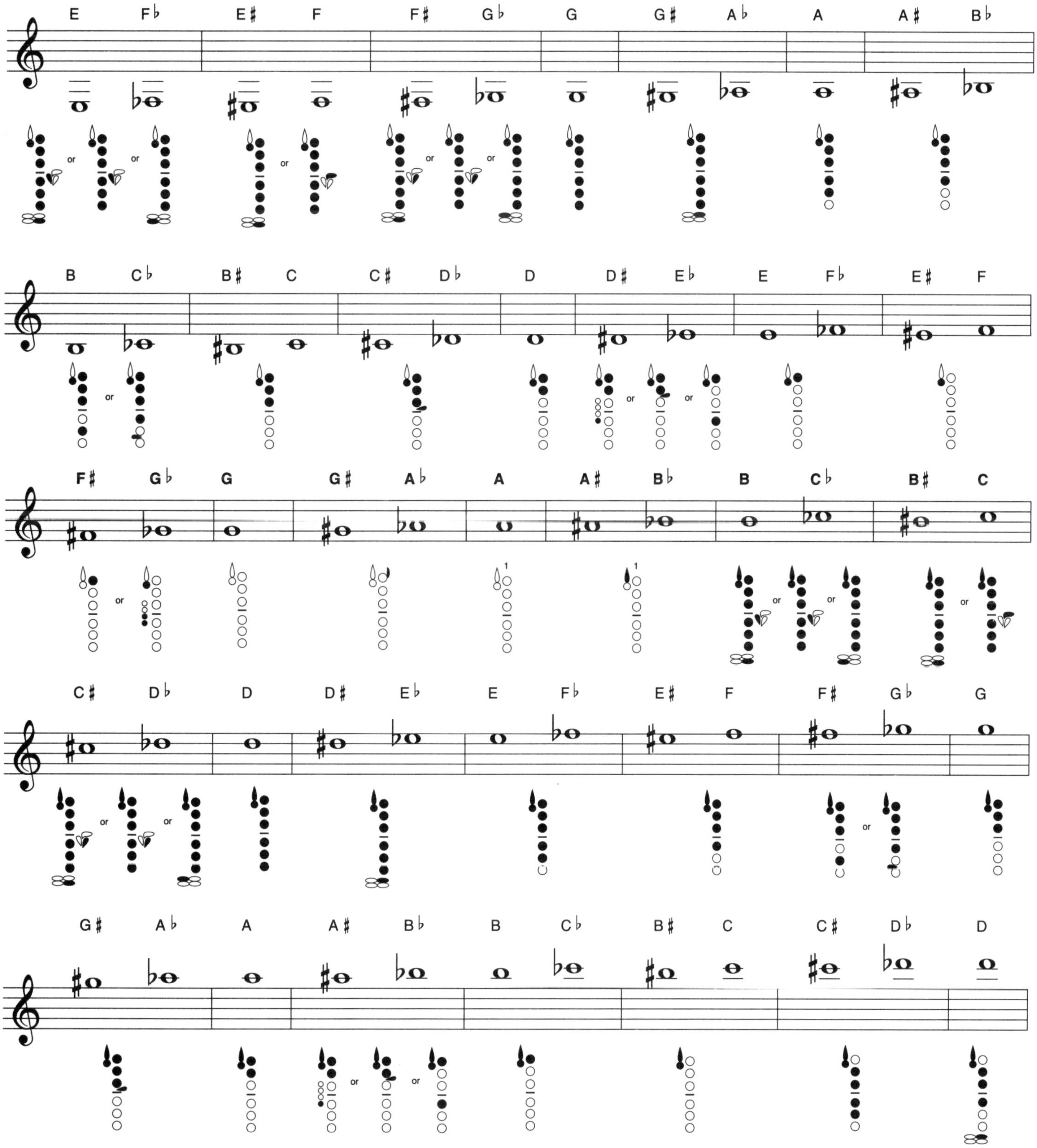
E F♭ E♯ F F♯ G♭ G G♯ A♭ A A♯ B♭
B C♭ B♯ C C♯ D♭ D D♯ E♭ E F♭ E♯ F
F♯ G♭ G G♯ A♭ A A♯ B♭ B C♭ B♯ C
C♯ D♭ D D♯ E♭ E F♭ E♯ F F♯ G♭ G
G♯ A♭ A A♯ B♭ B C♭ B♯ C C♯ D♭ D
or
1